The Salvation of Mankind by Jesus Christ

A Fresh Perspective

By

Kenny Dickerson

Copyright © 2003 by Kenny Dickerson

The Salvation of Mankind by Jesus Christ
by Kenny Dickerson

Printed in the United States of America

ISBN 1-591609-15-1

All rights reserved. No part of this publication may be reproduced or transmitted in any form or by any means without written permission of the publisher.

Unless otherwise indicated, Bible quotations are taken from the King James Version.

Xulon Press
www.XulonPress.com

Xulon Press books are available in bookstores everywhere, and on the Web at www.XulonPress.com.

Contents

Introduction vii
    "All For You" – Jesus Christ

Author's Message..ix
    Does the church in America today look like the church that was described in the book of Acts? How about its pastors & priests & overseers, are they fulfilling their call?

Chapter 1 17
    The testimony of two believers, grandpa and me! My goodness have times changed, but Jesus Christ is the same yesterday, today and forever.

Chapter 2 29
    What is Salvation? Salvation defined.
        Salvation, deliverance, sin, Savior and redemption defined, 1828 vs. today.

Chapter 3...41
    How does one receive salvation? Salvation received.
        It's as simple as A-B-C, Ask-Believe-Confess.

Chapter 4...45
    How do we know if someone we care about is saved? The Salvation Test.
        "Every spirit that confesseth that Jesus Christ is come in the flesh is of God"

Chapter 5..51
Can we ever lose our salvation? If so, how? Is there anything else we need to do to be saved?
A look at some hard to understand scriptures and false teaching within the church, as well as a comparison of water baptism vs. spiritual baptism.

Chapter 6..65
Are there scriptures that might lead us to a different conclusion? A right dividing of the Word of God for brethren with a heart for Truth.
Faith without works, Belief without works, Profit and Rewards, Fruit, Babes in Christ what does it all mean?

Our Spiritual Conclusion

Endnotes...81
Study references and recommendations

All For You

Listen carefully, for in my Word are precious truths I wish to impart to you. Feast on my words, for they are light and life, and in them there is no darkness.

I am come a light into the world, that whosoever believeth on me should not abide in darkness. It is I who have redeemed you from death into life everlasting. I AM that I AM, now and forever.

I have exalted my Word above all my Name, all for you. I have set down my Word for you, I have poured out my life for you. I AM the one who loves you, the one who died for you, the one who lives evermore for you. Truly I say to you, greater love hath no man than this, that a man lay down his life for his friends. This I have done for you!

I have done ALL for you!

Behold, I stand at the door of all hearts, waiting patiently to be invited in. For those in whom I already dwell, continue to abide in me. Let not your heart stray, for perilous times are upon the earth. Seek me now with full assurance, knowing that I AM he who will sustain you and guide you and lead you into Truth.

Jesus Christ,
Savior of the world

The Salvation of Mankind by Jesus Christ
A Fresh Perspective

Author's Message: There are many promises presented in scripture for those who unconditionally love Jesus Christ. My hope is that these words of exhortation are just another step The Lord of our salvation uses to help your walk glorify and honor Him. May we all love Him the way He deserves to be loved.

The Christian church in America today is so focused on "secular political correctness" that it has forgotten how to teach the Word of God without fear and without compromise. Many clergy today fear that someone's feelings might be hurt, or fear that church goers might be offended, so much that they tend to sprinkle the Truth with compromise. They candy coat the bitter pill of judgment in the scriptures with the sweet sugar of compromise. In the end however, they make the same mistake that Cain made in his offering to Almighty God recorded in Genesis 4. Cain actually thought he was giving God a better offering than Abel gave because of all the work he had put into raising and cultivating the crops he offered. Cain's error was he did not make the offering the way God designed offerings to be made. He took it upon himself to give God something better than what God had already provided. When we teach doctrines differently than they are presented in scripture (with all written consequences attached) we become partakers of the same error that Cain made. What is worse is that the hearers of our message then go out and walk by the words of our mouth and commit sins which we are partakers of, simply because we did not teach **<u>only</u>** what the Bible passage said. If we only teach what the passage says then we allow the Holy Spirit to do the teaching in people's hearts.

Satan, the accuser of the brethren from Revelation 12:10 has had over 2,000 years to infiltrate and infect the church, our seminaries, and our leadership with false doctrine. The net result is a watered down gospel containing watered down doctrines, which are in part void of the Truth and sprinkled with compromise.

Moreover, the structure of the church in America in 2003 is a far cry from the church structure both designed and described in the book of Acts.

Witness:

> John 10:11-13 (KJV) "¹¹ I am the good shepherd: the good shepherd giveth his life for the sheep. ¹² But he that is an <u>hireling</u>, and not the shepherd, whose own the sheep are not, <u>seeth the wolf coming, and leaveth the sheep, and fleeth: and the wolf catcheth them, and scattereth the sheep</u>. ¹³ <u>The hireling fleeth, because he is an hireling, and careth not for the sheep</u>."

A hireling is someone who is hired or serves for wages. The passage says that when the hireling "sees the wolf coming, he leaves the sheep and runs away." He does this because he is paid to do a job; he is not paid to care for the sheep. The hireling is paid to oversee the sheep, see that they are fed, and keep them from getting themselves into danger. He is not paid to jeopardize his life for the sheep. In this passage, Jesus is speaking about pastors (hirelings) overseeing the church (sheep). Today, many of our pastors and priests are hirelings making over $100,000 per year as paid presidents of religious clubs.

How can a pastor who is a hireling living in the top one half of 1% of the American populace, relate to and oversee the vast majority of American or foreign believers who have far less social status? They reside on different sides of the track, yet both are saddled with the same carnal nature. The question is rhetorical and the answer in the Christian church is the same as the answer in secular America, they can't - at least not very well.

Additionally, the church in America has become "lukewarm" as prophesied by Jesus Christ.

> Revelation 3:15-17 (KJV) "[15] I know thy works, that thou art neither cold nor hot: I would thou wert cold or hot. [16] So then because thou art lukewarm, and neither cold nor hot, I will spue thee out of my mouth. [17] Because thou sayest, I am rich, and increased with goods, and have need of nothing; and knowest not that thou art wretched, and miserable, and poor, and blind, and naked:"

This lukewarm attitude leads to a lukewarm walk and causes many weaker brethren to remain indifferent to the condition of the body of Christ in America. There was a time in my life when I was indifferent to error being taught in the church. I believe my indifference and willingness to compromise the truth came in part from the material blessings I was receiving from doing business within our congregation. The Lord humbled my compromising walk by dropping my income from ~$10,000/month to ~$500/month, and I resorted to throwing newspapers to put food on the table for my family. Only then, at the depth of my carnal despair, did I see and understand how a significant gap in material wealth directly affects how carnal mankind relates to one another.

I used to believe I was able to sincerely relate to everyone, regardless of his or her social status. The fact is, I was ignorance swimming in the lukewarm waters of compromise. I was ignorant to the truth because I was willing to compromise the standard of what sustains a genuine relationship. I didn't mind fellowship with brethren who were neither cold nor hot because I was comfortable in that setting. I never felt judged for my lukewarm walk even though Jesus Christ my Lord was judging my walk the entire time calling me into the fire and more reliance and commitment to Him.

Lukewarm believers, like their congregations, are not set for the defense of the gospel – they are set to justify their lifestyle instead. The Lord Jesus Christ prefers that we are either hot or cold in our relationship with Him, but certainly not lukewarm.

Regardless of the state of the church in America today, I will rejoice, because Jesus Christ is preached here. Paul did the same as an example of exhortation to us in the book of Philippians.

> Philippians 1: 14-18 (KJV) "¹⁴ And many of the brethren in the Lord, waxing confident by my bonds, are much more bold to speak the word without fear. ¹⁵ Some indeed preach Christ even of <u>envy</u> and <u>strife</u>; and some also of good will: ¹⁶ The one preach Christ of <u>contention</u>, <u>not sincerely</u>, supposing to add affliction to my bonds: ¹⁷ But the other of love, knowing that I am set for the defense of the gospel. ¹⁸ What then? Notwithstanding, <u>every way</u>, whether <u>in pretence</u>, or in truth, Christ is preached; and **<u>I therein do rejoice, yea, and will rejoice</u>.**"

Even though some bold preachers in the first century taught the gospel of Jesus Christ in error – "contention, envy, strife, not sincerely and in pretence" the Apostle Paul still rejoiced in "every way" Christ was preached. He rejoiced merely because the gospel of Jesus Christ was being preached. Churches are no more perfect than the fallen humans who manage them or attend them. We all must keep striving to learn and walk closer to the Lord Jesus Christ.

I trust there are many reasons why Paul rejoiced even when Jesus Christ was taught with doctrinal error, but one seems overwhelming: Where Jesus Christ is preached there is hope. Hope not because a man is preaching, but because the Holy Ghost is teaching.

> John 14:26 (KJV) "26* But the Comforter, which is the Holy Ghost, whom the Father will send in my name, <u>he shall teach you</u> **all things**, and bring **all things** to your remembrance, whatsoever I have said unto you."

When pastors are preaching, the Holy Ghost is whispering in our ear in His still quiet voice the glorious message of Truth. Therefore we are called to get our doctrines right, heed His call on our life and promised if we will do God's will, we will know the truth of any doctrine.

> John 7:17 (KJV) "17 If any man <u>will do His will</u>, he shall know of the doctrine, whether it be of God, or whether I speak of myself."

Unfortunately, too many believers are unwilling to do God's will, especially if it means change in their lives. Some of what you are about to read may change your life. It contains biblical truth you may have never heard before or even considered about the Salvation of Mankind by Jesus Christ. I encourage you to pray, and ask God if every doctrine taught from these true stories are the Truth.

Many influences lead brethren away from the Truth. We all

must study the Word of God to be cleansed and discover what God the Father Almighty has intended for our lives, Truth or compromise.

> 2 Timothy 2:15 (KJV) "¹⁵ <u>Study</u> to shew thyself approved unto God, a workman that needeth not to be ashamed, <u>rightly dividing the word of truth</u>. ¹⁶ But shun profane and vain babblings: for <u>they will increase unto more ungodliness</u>."

> 1 Corinthians 2:9-10 (KJV) "⁹ But as it is written, Eye hath not seen, nor ear heard, neither have entered into the heart of man, the things which God hath prepared **for them that love him**. ¹⁰ But God hath revealed *them* unto us by his Spirit: for the Spirit searcheth all things, yea, the <u>deep things of God</u>."

Before we step into the "deep things of God" however, we must first come to unity in the first principals of the faith, including the doctrine of Christ and the many relevant issues surrounding His free and perfect gift.

> Hebrews 6:1 (KJV) "¹ Therefore <u>leaving the principles of the doctrine of Christ, let us go on</u> unto perfection; not laying again the foundation of repentance from dead works, and of faith toward God, ² Of the doctrine of baptisms, and of laying on of hands, and of resurrection of the dead, and of eternal judgment."

To begin our study, seeking to "show ourselves approved unto God a workman that needeth not be ashamed" (2 Timothy 2:15), let's examine five important questions:

The Salvation of Mankind by Jesus Christ

- [1]What is Salvation?
- [2]How does one receive salvation?
- [3]How do we know if someone we care about is saved?
- [4]Can we ever lose our salvation? If so, how?
- [5]Is there anything else we need to do to be saved (be baptized, do good works, etc.)?
- [6]Are there scriptures that seem to lead us to a different conclusion? Plus more evidence.

Chapter 1

Two Believer's Testimonies

GRANDPA'S QUESTION AND THE HOLY SPIRIT'S ANSWER

A few years back I was asked by my grandfather to officiate his funeral service. Grandpa's rough persona was often viewed as grumpy, yet inside he was a lovable old man. I never knew exactly where his persona came from; I guess I never really thought that much about it. Prior to this time grandpa and I had never discussed anything about Jesus Christ openly. All the things a young Christian man desires to discuss with a wiser, more seasoned believer were never discussed. Our visits to grandpa's home were usually around the holidays and would consist of playing cards, discussing the trials and tribulations of the Denver Broncos, politics, and dinner. The deeper topics of Christianity just never came up in conversation.

One fine day things changed. Family members were concerned about grandpa's salvation. In fact, some of them were sure he was saved and some were sure he was not saved. Regardless of what they thought, nobody knew how to ask him. I guess grandpa was a bit intimidating in the way he formed and expressed his opinions. His opinion was usually the first, sometimes the middle, and almost always the last.

How do we approach an older man whom we were taught to honor and respect with such a personal question? What do we say? "So grandpa, speaking about those Broncos, are you saved? Do you believe in Jesus Christ? Is Jesus Christ your Lord and Savior?" This was all very awkward to me because grandpa was very ill and conversation with him was at a premium. I didn't want to talk about anything he didn't want to talk about, yet the Holy Spirit was leading me into a head-on collision with God's call on my life.

Grandpa was suffering with congestive heart failure, and he had reached the end of his days when he and grandma approached me about the idea of officiating his funeral service. He was home and waiting for death to come, there was nothing else the doctors could do for him. Only hospice care, nurses and medication filled his remaining time on earth. He seemed to be hesitantly waiting at death's door. As a result of his condition some family members felt a little uncomfortable asking the difficult question and understandably so. Whom did they ask to follow through with this most undesirable task? Why me of course, through my mother...

Mother came to me a few days before grandpa's death and sat me down for a little story. It went something like this; "Kenny, grandpa's children (mother included) are concerned that grandpa isn't saved!" I was a little taken back at her statement, thinking to myself, what do they expect me to do about it? I had mixed feelings of confusion and frustration that Christian family members would dare judge another man's salvation. Later in my walk I learned that we are all called to judge in righteousness, comparing everything with the Word of God, "spiritual things (life and it's events) with spiritual (the Word of God)."

1 Corinthians 2:12-15 (KJV) "¹² Now we have received, not the spirit of the world, but the spirit which is of God; that we might know the things that are freely given to us of God. ¹³ Which things also we speak, not in the words which man's wisdom teacheth, but which the Holy Ghost teacheth; <u>comparing spiritual things with spiritual</u>. ¹⁴ But the natural man receiveth not the things of the Spirit of God: for they are foolishness unto him: neither can he know *them*, because they are spiritually discerned. ¹⁵ But **he that is spiritual judgeth all things**, yet he himself is judged of no man."

At this time in my walk, however, the thought of one believer passing judgment upon another believer really upset me. Nonetheless, I love, honor, and respect my mother very much. After all it was her daily prayer and agape love that helped lead me to my Lord and Savior, Jesus Christ. So when mom asked if I would talk to grandpa, I couldn't refuse her, especially in this time of desperate concern. The scriptures taught me:

Exodus 20:12 (KJV) "¹² Honor thy father and thy mother: that thy days may be long upon the land which the Lord thy God giveth thee."

The scripture says honor thy father and thy mother. Why? That we might live long upon the land given unto us by God. In fact, this is the only commandment in Exodus 20 which has a reward directly attached to it. Soon thereafter, the Holy Ghost moved upon me, and honoring my mother's wishes became paramount in my heart.

I remember wondering, how could there be any question about grandpa's salvation knowing he raised four sincere Christian children and married a Christian woman? On the other hand, how could he be saved if his own children didn't know whether he was a believer and saved? At the height of my confusion, mom shared an amazing story later expanded by grandma.

When my mother and her siblings were growing up they lived in a small town in central Nebraska. This little town had a population of, let's say, four hundred for the story's sake. This tiny little town had two churches, a grocery store, a gas station, and a liquor store. It just so happened that grandpa owned the liquor store. On Sunday mornings the children went off to church at one of the two churches for Sunday school, but grandpa and grandma stayed home.

Unfortunately, deacons in these churches expressed their concern that mom and the kids shouldn't be allowed to attend vacation Bible School. They cited "sins of the father" as reason for their belief, and they would not let grandpa attend their assembly because he owned the one and only liquor store in town. Ultimately, the children were allowed to attend yet not encouraged to do so. I suppose they felt sorry for the kids and hoped the rest of the family, with the push of the churches, would convert my "heathen" grandpa.

My "heathen" grandpa, for obvious reasons, hated the two churches and swore he would never set foot in a church again. He also told me that he would never allow a minister to bury him. It seems he had good reason; because not one, but both of the town's self-proclaimed "God fearing" ministers would purchase liquor from grandpa's liquor store. You might be thinking, "so what's the big deal, ministers all over the world drink an occasional glass of wine at dinner, or on special occasions, right?" It wasn't the purchasing the booze that put grandpa over the edge. These men both made grandpa put liquor in brown paper bags and deliver it out the back door of his liquor store so nobody in town would see them buy the booze and judge them unrighteous. Can you imagine the hypocrisy? Grandpa sure could – and it changed his life forever and specifically his attitude toward the church and it's ministers.

The Salvation of Mankind by Jesus Christ

When mom and grandpa told me their own versions of this story, things started making a bit more sense and the big picture of grandpa's life started coming into focus. I could see why the kids were so unsure and why they felt so much concern; after all, they witnessed frustration toward the church burn in grandpa for over half a century. Finally, I too understood, at least to some degree, what was going on in grandpa's mind? Soon thereafter grandpa and I had an enlightening conversation that, for me, was life changing.

We were sitting in the living room at my grandparent's home having a "casual conversation" about death (if talking about death with a dying man is ever casual). In an inquisitive manner I asked grandpa if he feared death. In classic grandpa style he responded, "Hell no, why should I, it's dying that hurts." I continued, inquiring about how he felt; was the morphine working? could he feel his legs? etc... By this time he had no feeling in his feet. They were basically dead, and death was slowly moving up the rest of his body.

Then, I was moved by the Holy Ghost to just ask the question. I said, "Grandpa, the family is concerned whether or not you are saved and they sent me to find out." Grandpa replied, "What the hell would they worry about that for?" There was a long pause, and I could sense his spirit was stirring...then he continued, "I mean, how do you know? How do you really know if you're saved?" he asked. "I mean, nobody ever died and came back to tell us about it, how do you know?" At this point in our conversation the Holy Spirit moved on me again and gave me one scripture for grandpa, a passage I'll never forget:

Romans 10:9 (KJV) "9 That if thou shalt **confess** with thy mouth the Lord Jesus, and shalt **believe** in thine heart that God hath raised him from the dead, **thou shalt be saved**."

That was it! That was the Holy Spirit's answer for grandpa's question. If he **confessed** with his mouth that Jesus is Lord (his Lord), and he **believed** in his heart that God (the Father Almighty) had raised Him (Jesus Christ) from the dead, **he would be saved**, period.

The Encarta® World English Dictionary © 1999 Microsoft Corporation defines **Believe** as:

1. to accept that something is true or real
2. to accept that somebody is telling the truth
3. to accept that somebody or something has a particular quality or ability
4. to be of the opinion that something exists or is a reality, especially when there is no absolute proof of its existence or reality
5. to be confident that somebody or something is good, or will be effective
6. to be of the opinion that something is right or beneficial, and, usually, to act in accordance with that belief
7. <u>to have a religious belief</u>

and **Confess** as:

1. to admit openly a wrongdoing, crime, or error
2. to admit the truth of something, for example, something that might reflect badly or be embarrassing
3. to reveal sins to a priest or to God and ask for forgiveness
4. to listen to somebody's confession of sins
5. <u>to declare faith or belief in something or somebody (archaic)</u>

Re-read the 1999 World English Dictionary definition of the word "Believe." Now let us look at how the exact same word was defined in America using the **American Dictionary of the English Language by Noah Webster in 1828**:

> "**Believe:** To credit upon the authority or testimony of another; to be persuaded of the truth of something upon the declaration of another, or upon evidence furnished by reasons, arguments, and deductions of the mind, or by other circumstances, than personal knowledge. When we **believe** upon the authority of another, we always put confidence in his veracity. When we **believe** upon the authority of reasoning, arguments, or concurrence of facts and circumstances, we rest our conclusions upon their strength or probability, their agreement with our own experience and conclusions.
> 2. To expect or hope with confidence; to trust.
> "<u>I had fainted, unless I had **believed** to see the goodness of the Lord in the land of the living." Psalms xxvii.</u>
> **Believe:** To have a firm persuasion of anything. In some cases, to have full persuasion, approaching to certainty; in others, more doubt is implied. <u>It is often followed by in or on, especially in the scriptures. To believe in, is to hold as the object of faith. "Ye believe in God, believe also in me." John xiv.</u> To believe on, is to trust to place full confidence in, to rest upon with faith. "<u>To them gave he power to become sons of God, even to them that believe on his name." John i.</u>"

The 1828 dictionary goes on to describe the word "believe" as it is used in theology, in popular use and familiar discourse. My goodness have times changed!

Has America changed over the last 175 years toward God, or away from Him? It is almost unbelievable to think that only 175 years ago that which defined the basis of American life was what the Bible says, not what secular philosophy, or political correctness says. After reviewing just a few dictionary definitions between 1828 and 1999, it seems that by the year 1999 Americans have become so intelligent that they no longer need to define things in life by what God says about them. Nevertheless, only the scriptures stand true.

Back to the Story

All grandpa had to do was 1. <u>Believe</u> Jesus is Lord, and 2. <u>Confess</u> that belief to someone, and he would be saved. It's a simple two-part process! The scripture continues:

> Romans 10:10-13 (KJV) "¹⁰ For with the <u>heart</u> man **believeth** <u>unto righteousness</u>; and with the <u>mouth</u> **confession** <u>is made unto salvation</u>. ¹¹ For the scripture saith, whosoever **believeth** on him shall not be ashamed. ¹² For there is no difference between the Jew and the Greek: for the same Lord over all is rich unto all that call upon him. ¹³ For whosoever shall call upon the name of the Lord <u>shall be saved</u>."

After I spoke those words to grandpa, he turned to me and confessed his belief. Grandpa was saved indeed, praise the Lord. How do we know he was saved? Because he **confessed** with his mouth and **believed** in his heart that Jesus is Lord and God raised Him from the dead. The scripture provides no other conditions for salvation. I knew from that moment on that my grandpa would soon be in the presence of our sweet Lord, our great God and savior, Jesus Christ. I was finally 100% sure of his salvation. I couldn't wait to pass on the good news.

A couple of related scriptures including things we can and cannot say with the Spirit of God in us:

> ∞ John 11: 25-27 (KJV) "²⁵ Jesus said unto her, I am the resurrection, and the life: he that believeth in me, though he were dead, yet shall he live: ²⁶ And whosoever liveth and believeth in me shall never die. Believest thou this? ²⁷ She saith unto him, Yea, Lord: **I believe** that thou art the Christ, the Son of God, which should come into the world."

This woman, like my grandpa, was saved because she believed and confessed Jesus Christ as her Lord.

> ∞ 1 Corinthians 12:3 (KJV) "³ Wherefore I give you to understand, that no man speaking by the Spirit of God **calleth Jesus accursed**: and *that* no man can say that **Jesus is the Lord**, but by the Holy Ghost."

A man cannot say Jesus is the Lord, but by the Holy Ghost. The Holy Ghost is only with believers. Also, no man speaking by the Spirit of God can say Jesus is accursed. If a man or woman has the Spirit of God with them, they cannot say "Jesus is accursed" and mean it!

Salvation is a free and perfect gift from God the Father Almighty, thanks to His son Jesus Christ's death on the cross. Any requirement on our part would cheapen what Jesus Christ did by dying on a cross for all mankind. The scripture also says:

> James 1:17 (KJV) "¹⁷ Every good gift and every perfect gift (salvation and more) is from above, and cometh down from the Father of lights, with whom is no variableness **(variation)** neither shadow of turning."

I'd say Jesus Christ is the best gift of all time. A good and perfect gift.

KENNY'S SALVATION TESTIMONY

In 1976, during Resurrection Sunday vacation (Easter to secular society - Easter is a pagan goddess of fertility), my family went to Mesa, Arizona to visit my paternal grandparents.

> According to the American Dictionary of the English Language by Noah Webster in 1828, **Easter** is defined as follows: "supposed to be from *Eostre*, the goddess of love or Venus of the North, in honor of whom a festival was celebrated by our pagan ancestors, in April; whence this month was called *Eostermonath*. *Eostre* is supposed by Beda and others to be the Astarte of the Sidonians.
>
> A festival of the Christian church observed in commemoration of our Savior's resurrection. It answers to the pascha or Passover of the Hebrews, and most nations still give it this name, pascha, pask, paque."

The Roman Catholic church began the "Easter" tradition in the church as an answer to the pagan celebration of Eostre. We should ask ourselves: Since when does Almighty God desire us to take pagan practices and make them Christian? We've done the same thing with Christmas. See Jeremiah chapter 10.

Resurrection Sunday was an important day for my mother, and what was about to happen would change the lives of my entire family for eternity.

I was a sophomore attending Columbine High School in Littleton, Colorado, and I was very unhappy. I didn't like myself much, I didn't like my family, I didn't like my school or my classmates or my teachers, and I especially didn't care for God. I thought "How could a real God make my life so miserable?" Looking back, I see that I was a spoiled rotten little brat and didn't have a clue, but I had everything materially a young man could ever want. To this day

The Salvation of Mankind by Jesus Christ

I wonder in amazement how my parents tolerated such a self-centered adolescent. (Notice all the I's in this paragraph, it gives the reader an indication as to where my focus was directed. On Me!)

I did not trust anybody, with the part time exception of my parents. Sometimes I felt mom was by my side, and with dad I just knew he would be available only if things got too tough. By this time in my life I had quit all the team sports I so dearly loved, football, baseball and basketball. I had decided in my own prideful mind that I couldn't trust my teammates to get me where I wanted to go, so I switched to tennis and wrestling in order to "control my own destination". Like the pharaohs of Egypt I was in control, or so I thought.

I remember very little about this particular vacation other than I really didn't want to be there. God, however, had another agenda. Grandma and grandpa lived in a small retirement community called Sun Lakes, Arizona. There was a small chapel within the gated community, which we attended for Resurrection Sunday services. I can't remember much about the service, but I do remember that the pastor was a "hell, fire and brimstone maniac," at least that was my prejudging impression. As the service came to a close, the pastor addressed visitors from out of town. He said "If you're here visiting from out of town I have a question for you. If you get on that plane to go home tomorrow and it crashes, where will you go? Will you go to heaven and be with Jesus or will you go to hell and spend eternity with satan? Do you really know for sure?"

Shortly thereafter, the pastor led an altar call inviting everybody who didn't know for sure where they would go to come down and ask Jesus Christ into their lives. A few people went forward, and that's when things got a little weird.

I felt such a strong pull on my body that I actually thought someone or something was physically pulling me out of my pew seat. I resisted, protecting my ego and did not go forward. A short while later we all hopped into the golf cart and went home.

After church we would typically talk about the service and discuss the sermon over brunch, this time however would be very different. Grandma asked us all what we thought about the service and the pastor, etc.? I was first to respond…I told the family what had happened to me; how I felt like I was being pulled right out of my seat, I told them how I had an incredible desire to go down for that altar call. As you can imagine my evangelical grandmother started getting excited.

Shortly after I described my experience, my father joined in saying "that's funny, I felt the exact same thing." Moments later, my younger brother proclaimed "me too!" We all looked around at each other in amazement. That was the long pause grandma needed, she picked up the phone, called the pastor and told him to stay right there, we were coming back and he had some more work to do. She loaded us all up in the golf cart and back to church we went.

When we arrived back at church, the pastor spoke with us briefly all together. We got on our knees and we all three repented of our sins and asked Jesus Christ to forgive us. How's that for a three in one miracle? Grandma wasn't the only one relieved; can you imagine what life was like for my mother who had three testosterone loaded, unsaved, prideful males to care for and love on a daily basis.

Only by the grace of God could she find the stamina to deal with that much pride in one household. I remember one night catching my mom praying before bedtime and I actually asked her why she did that and she replied that she prayed daily. I spent the next 30 minutes challenging her that she had to be lying because nobody in this world prays every day. As I look back on my life I praise God that He didn't take me then and I wonder why He allowed such "prideful ignorance" to live in me. I suppose mom's prayers really worked, I'm sure more than just a few of her prayers were directed my way.

Chapter 2

Salvation Defined

What is salvation?

Nelsons Illustrated Bible Dictionary defines salvation as "**deliverance** from the power of **sin; redemption**."

Sin is "lawlessness or the transgression of God's will, either by omitting to do what God's law requires or by doing what God's law forbids.

> 1 John 3:4 (KJV) "⁴Whosoever committeth sin transgresseth also the law: for <u>**sin** is the transgression of the law</u>."

The transgression can occur in **thought** (i.e. things we think, like hatred, anger without a cause, malice, etc.).

> 1 John 3:15 (KJV) "¹⁵Whosoever <u>hateth</u> his brother is a murderer: and ye know that no murderer hath eternal life abiding in him."

> Matthew 5:27-28 (KJV) "²⁷Ye have heard that it was said by

them of old time, Thou shalt not commit adultery: ²⁸But I say unto you, That whosoever looketh on a woman to <u>lust</u> after her hath committed adultery with her already in his heart."

The transgression can occur in our **words** (i.e. things we say).

Matthew 5:22 (KJV) "²²But I say unto you, That whosoever is angry with his brother without a cause shall be in danger of the judgment: and whosoever shall **<u>say</u>** <u>to his brother, Raca,</u> shall be in danger of the council: but whosoever shall **<u>say</u>**, <u>Thou fool</u>, shall be in danger of hell fire."

Raca means … to be empty, i.e. a senseless, empty headed man. It was a term of reproach used among the Jews in the time of Christ.

The transgression can occur in our **deeds** (i.e. things we do, our actions).

Romans 1:32 (KJV) "³²Who knowing the judgment of God, that they which <u>commit</u> such things are worthy of death, not only **do** the same, but have pleasure in them that **do** them."

The transgression can occur in our **motives** (i.e. reason behind our actions).

1 Chronicles 28:9 And thou, Solomon my son, know thou the God of thy father, and serve him with a <u>perfect heart and with a willing mind</u>: for the LORD searcheth all hearts, and understandeth all the <u>imaginations of the thoughts</u>: if thou seek him, he will be found of thee; but if thou forsake him, he will cast thee off for ever.

Once again, to demonstrate how far America has veered off course, let us look at the definitions of "Salvation, Savior, Sin and Redemption" found in American History using the American Dictionary of the English Language by Noah Webster in 1828:

Salvation "1. The act of saving; preservation from destruction, danger or great calamity. 2. Appropriately in theology, the redemption of man from the bondage of sin and liability to eternal death, and the conferring on Him everlasting happiness. This is the *great salvation*. 3. Deliverance from enemies; victory. Exodus xiv. 4. Remission of sins, or saving graces. Luke xix. 5 The author of man's salvation. Psalms xxvii. 6. A term of praise or benediction. Revelation xix."

Savior "One that saves or preserves; but properly applied only to Jesus Christ, the Redeemer, who has opened the way to everlasting salvation by his obedience and death, and who is therefore called *the Savior*, by way of distinction, *the Savior* of men, *the Savior* of the world. General Washington may be called the saver, but not the *savior* of his country."

Sin "1. The voluntary departure of a moral agent from a known rule of rectitude or duty, prescribed by God; any voluntary transgression of divine law, or violation of a divine command; a wicked act; iniquity. *Sin* is either a positive act in which a known divine law is violated, or it is the voluntary neglect to obey a positive divine command, or a rule of duty clearly implied in such command. *Sin* comprehends not actions only, but neglect of known duty, all evil thoughts, purposes, words and desires, whatever is contrary to God's commands or law. 1 John iii. Matthew xv. James iv."

Sinners neither enjoy the pleasures of sin, nor the peace of piety. Rob Hall.

Among divines, sin is *original* or *actual*. *Actual sin*, above defined, is the act of a moral agent in violating a known rule of duty. *Original sin*, as generally understood, is native depravity of heart to the divine will, that corruption of nature or deterioration of the moral character of man, which is supposed to be the effect of Adam's apostasy; and which manifests itself in moral agents by positive acts of disobedience to the divine will, or by voluntary neglect to comply with the express commands of God, which require that we should love God with all the heart an soul and strength and mind, and our neighbor as ourselves. This native depravity or alienation of affections from God and His law is supposed to be what the Apostle calls the *carnal mind*, or *mindedness*, which is enmity against God, and is therefore denominated *sin* or *sinfulness*.

Unpardonable sin, or blasphemy against the Holy Spirit, is supposed to be a malicious and obstinate rejection of Christ and the gospel plan of salvation, or a contemptuous resistance made to the influences and convictions of the Holy Spirit. Mathew xii.

2. A sin-offering; an offering made to atone for sin.

He hath made Him to be *sin* for us, who knew no *sin*. 2 Corinthians v.

3. A man enormously wicked. Shakespeare.

Sin differs from *crime*, not in nature, but in application. That which is a *crime* against society is *sin* against

God."

Isn't it amazing how much scripture was quoted in the 1828 definitions? Can you imagine a professor today quoting from a dictionary, a definition that contained so many references to Jesus Christ and the books of the Holy Bible? Especially in light of the authority such definitions give to Him.

For a more in-depth study about the effects of sin in our lives, King David's realization about his own sins shortly after his adulterous transgression with Bathsheba and subsequent murder of her husband is very revealing:

∞ Psalm 51:1-11: (KJV) "<<A Psalm of David, when Nathan the prophet came unto him, after he had gone in to Bathsheba.>> Have mercy upon me, O God, according to thy loving-kindness: according unto the multitude of thy tender mercies blot out my transgressions. ²Wash me thoroughly from mine iniquity, and cleanse me from my sin. ³For I acknowledge my transgressions: and my sin *is* ever before me. ⁴Against thee, thee only, have I sinned, and done *this* evil in thy sight: that thou mightest be justified when thou speakest, *and* be clear when thou judgest. ⁵Behold, I was shapen in iniquity; and in sin did my mother conceive me. ⁶Behold, thou desirest truth in the inward parts: and in the hidden *part* thou shalt make me to know wisdom. ⁷Purge me with hyssop, and I shall be clean: wash me, and I shall be whiter than snow. ⁸Make me to hear joy and gladness; *that* the bones *which* thou hast broken may rejoice. ⁹Hide thy face from my sins, and blot out all mine iniquities. ¹⁰Create in me a clean heart, O God; and renew a right spirit within me. ¹¹Cast me not away from thy presence; and take not thy holy spirit from me."

David saw that his sins were against God and Him only. If we could all understand that we were created to live life in such a way as to show the world the true character of God – His love, His grace, His mercy, His holiness, etc., we would see our sins as King David saw his own sins. David surely understood God's will for his life, even when he wasn't quite performing up to God's standards.

Mankind was created without sin, morally upright and inclined to do "good"

> Ecclesiastes 7:29 (KJV) "29 Lo, this only have I found, that God hath made man upright; but they have sought out many inventions."

But sin entered into human experience when Adam and Eve violated the direct command of God by eating the forbidden fruit in the center of the Garden of Eden.

> Genesis 3:6 (KJV) "6 And when the woman saw that the tree was good for food, and that it was pleasant to the eyes, and a tree to be desired to make one wise, she took of the fruit thereof, and did eat, and gave also unto her husband with her; and he did eat."

Because Adam was the head and representative of the whole human race, his sin affected all future generations.

> Romans 5:12-18 (KJV) "12 Wherefore, as by one man sin entered into the world, and death by sin; and so death passed upon all men, for that all have sinned: 13 (For until the law sin was in the world: but sin is not imputed when there is no law. 14 Nevertheless death reigned from Adam to Moses, even over them that had not sinned after the similitude of Adam's transgression, who is the figure of him that was to come. 15 But not

as the offence, so also *is* the free gift. For if through the offence of one many be dead, much more the grace of God, and the gift by grace, *which is* by one man, Jesus Christ, hath abounded unto many. ¹⁶ And not as *it was* by one that sinned, *so is* the gift: for the judgment *was* by one to condemnation, but the free gift *is* of many offences unto justification. ¹⁷ For if by one man's offence death reigned by one; much more they which receive abundance of grace and of the gift of righteousness shall reign in life by one, Jesus Christ.) ¹⁸ Therefore as by the offence of one *judgment came* upon all men to condemnation; even so <u>by the righteousness of one *the free gift came* upon all men unto justification of life</u>."

No person is free from sin, no man is just and we shouldn't even think such foolishness for the scripture says:

Romans 3:23-25, 28 (KJV) "²³ For <u>all have sinned</u>, and come short of the glory of God; ²⁴Being justified freely (without any cost to us) by his grace through the redemption that is in Christ Jesus: ²⁵Whom God hath set forth to be a propitiation (mercy seat) through faith in his blood, to declare (demonstrate) his righteousness for the remission (passing over of) of sins that are past, through the forbearance of God. ²⁸Therefore <u>we conclude that man is justified</u> (declared righteous) <u>by faith</u> without (apart from) the deeds of the law."

Ecclesiastes 7:20 (KJV) "²⁰ For there is not a just man upon earth, that doeth good, <u>and sinneth not</u>."

1 John 1:8 (KJV) "⁸ If we say that we have no sin, we deceive ourselves, and <u>the truth is not in us</u>."

Since the fall of mankind, all who were born thereafter are born into sin (Romans 3:23). We do not have a choice. We do, however, have a choice to do something about our sinful nature. We can seek redemption from the Creator of the universe, Jesus Christ. Not only is Jesus Christ the Creator of all that we know, He holds everything together, the world, the universe, everything.

> Genesis 1:1 (KJV) "<u>¹ In the beginning</u> God created the heaven and the earth."

> John 1:1-3 (KJV) "<u>¹ In the beginning was the Word</u>, and <u>the Word was with God</u>, and <u>the Word was God</u>. ² The same was in the beginning with God. ³ <u>All things were made by him</u>; and without him was not any thing made that was made."

Jesus Christ is the written Word of God, in Greek, the "logos." All things were made by Him, and only in Him do we have redemption.

> Colossians 1:13-17 (KJV) "¹³ Who hath delivered us from the power of darkness, and hath translated *us* into the <u>kingdom of his dear Son</u>: ¹⁴ <u>In whom we have **redemption** through his blood, even the forgiveness of sins</u>: ¹⁵ Who is the image of the invisible God, the firstborn of every creature: ¹⁶ For <u>by him were all things created</u>, that are in heaven, and that are in earth, visible and invisible, whether *they be* thrones, or dominions, or principalities, or powers: all things were created by him, and for him: ¹⁷ And he is before all things, and <u>by him all things consist</u>."

> Ephesians 3:9 (KJV) "⁹ And to make all *men* see what *is* the fellowship of the mystery, which from the beginning of the world hath been hid in God, <u>who created all things by Jesus Christ</u>:"

Hebrews 1:2 (KJV) "¹ God, who at sundry times and in divers manners spake in time past unto the fathers by the prophets, ² Hath in these last days spoken unto us by *his* Son, whom he hath appointed heir of all things, <u>by whom also he made the worlds</u>;"

God the Father Almighty in heaven truly loves us all. He loves us so much that he gave His only begotten Son for us:

John 3:16-18 (KJV) ¹⁶ For <u>God so loved the world, that He gave His only begotten Son, that whosoever **believeth** in Him should not perish, but have everlasting life.</u> ¹⁷ For God sent not His Son into the world to condemn the world; but that the world through Him might be saved (redeemed, delivered). ¹⁸ He that believeth on Him is not condemned: but he that believeth not is condemned already, because he hath not believed in the name of the only begotten Son of God.

Redemption is "<u>deliverance by payment of a price</u>," according to Nelson's Illustrated Bible Dictionary.

Jesus Christ paid the price for everyone's sin when he chose to die on the cross for our redemption. He purchased us back for a price, his blood on the cross.

1 Peter 1:18-19 (KJV) "¹⁸ Forasmuch as ye know that <u>ye were not **redeemed** with corruptible things</u>, *as* silver and gold, from your vain conversation *received* by tradition from your fathers; ¹⁹ But <u>with the precious blood of Christ</u>, as of a lamb without blemish and without spot:"

We are no longer our own, but His servants by our choice and His grace. We are a purchased possession belonging to Jesus Christ.

By His grace we still have the freedom to make choices, good and bad. All that we are belongs to God, both our body and our spirit.

> Acts 20:28 (KJV) "28 Take heed therefore unto yourselves, and to all the flock, over the which the Holy Ghost hath made you overseers, to <u>feed the church of God, which he hath</u> **<u>purchased</u>** <u>with his own blood</u>."

> Ephesians 1:12-14(KJV) " 12 That we should be to the praise of his glory, who first trusted in Christ. 13 In whom ye also *trusted*, after that ye heard the word of truth, the gospel of your salvation: in whom also after that ye believed, ye were sealed with that holy Spirit of promise, 14 <u>Which is the earnest of our inheritance until the</u> **<u>redemption of the purchased possession</u>**, unto the praise of his glory.

> 1 Corinthians 6:19-20 (KJV) "19 What? know ye not that your body is the temple of the Holy Ghost *which is* in you, which ye have of God, and ye are not your own? 20 For **<u>ye are bought with a price</u>**<u>: therefore glorify God in</u> **<u>your body</u>**<u>, and in</u> **<u>your spirit, which are God's</u>**."

One last time, and as yet one more witness to the ignorance and compromise in America today, let us look at the definition of "Redemption" found in American History using the American Dictionary of the English Language by Noah Webster in 1828:

> "**Redemption** 1. Repurchase of captured goods or prisoners; the act of procuring the deliverance of persons or things from the possession and power of captors by the payment of an equivalent; ransom; release; as the redemption of prisoners taken in war; the redemption of a ship and cargo. 2.

Deliverance from bondage, distress, or from liability to any evil of forfeiture, either by money, labor or other means. 3. Repurchase, as of lands alienated. Leviticus xxv. Jeremiah xxxii. 4. the liberation of an estate from a mortgage; or the purchase of the right to reenter upon it by paying the principal sum for which it was mortgaged, with interest and cost; also, the right of redeeming and re-entering. 5. Repurchase of notes, bills or other evidence of debt by paying their value in specie to their holders.

<u>In theology, the purchase of God's favor by the death and sufferings of Christ; the ransom or deliverance of sinners from the bondage of sin and the penalties of God's violated law by the atonement of Christ."</u>

If you feel drawn to God now, accept His free and perfect gift, don't wait another minute or read another page before you do. If you do not act now, you may never get another chance. The Holy Bible says…

"No man can come to Me (Jesus), except the Father which hath sent Me (Jesus) draw him: and I (Jesus) will raise him up at the last day" John 6:44 (KJV).

If you feel God the Father drawing you to Jesus Christ His son, please don't waste another moment. Bow your head in prayer, or raise up your hands and ask Jesus Christ to forgive your sins, tell Him you Believe He is Lord, and Confess that God raised Him from the dead. You will never be the same again; you will be changed for all eternity. It is the gift of God so that no man can boast of his own goodness.

Ephesians 2:8-9 (KJV) ⁸ For by grace are ye saved through faith; and that not of yourselves: it is <u>the **gift** of God</u>: ⁹ Not of works, lest any man should boast.

Chapter 3

Salvation Received

²**How does one receive salvation?**

Simply ASK your Creator.

Matthew 7:7-8 (KJV) "⁷ **Ask**, and it shall be given you; **seek**, and ye shall find; **knock**, and it shall be opened unto you: ⁸ For every one that asketh receiveth; and he that seeketh findeth; and to him that knocketh it shall be opened".

Just ask God to save you, seek Him, and knock at His door. He will give unto you salvation, you will find the Truth in Him, and the door to spiritual enlightenment will be opened for you to enter into His rest. His Word is His promise. It's that simple, His free and perfect gift to you requires nothing more than **believing** in Him and **confessing** that belief to others.

Jesus Christ is our all-in-all, our mere confession results in forgiveness and cleansing:

1 John 1:9-10 (KJV) "⁹ If <u>we **confess** our sins, he is faithful</u>

and just to **forgive** us our sins, and to cleanse us from all unrighteousness. 10 If we say that we have not sinned, we make him a liar, and his word is not in us."

Acts 16:29-31 (KJV) "29 Then he called for a light, and sprang in, and came trembling, and fell down before Paul and Silas, 30 And brought them out, and said, Sirs, **what must I do to be saved?** 31 And they said, **Believe** on the Lord Jesus Christ, and **thou shalt be saved**, and thy house."

It is God's will that all would be saved and come to the knowledge of the truth.

1 Timothy 2:3-6 (KJV) "3 For this is good and acceptable in the sight of God our Saviour; 4 **Who will have all men to be saved, and to come unto the knowledge of the truth.** 5 For there is one God, and one mediator between God and men, the man Christ Jesus; 6 Who gave himself a ransom for all, to be testified in due time."

Reality however, is that too many of us are living unholy lives and are thus forever learning, but never coming to the knowledge of truth. 2 Timothy 3:1-8 gives us an indication that we may very well be living in the last of the last days.

2 Timothy 3:1-8 (KJV) "1 This know also, that **in the last days perilous times shall come.** 2 For men shall be lovers of their own selves, covetous, boasters, proud, blasphemers, disobedient to parents, unthankful, unholy, 3 Without natural affection, trucebreakers, false accusers, incontinent, fierce, despisers of those that are good, 4 Traitors, heady, high-minded, lovers of pleasures more than lovers of God; 5 Having a form of godliness,

<u>but denying the power thereof: from such turn away.</u> ⁶ For of this sort are they which creep into houses, and lead captive silly women laden with sins, led away with divers lusts, ⁷ **Ever learning, and never able to come to the knowledge of the truth.** ⁸ Now as Jannes and Jambres withstood Moses, so do these also resist the truth: men of corrupt minds, reprobate concerning the faith."

The spiritual truth and knowledge of any doctrine is open and available to us, **IF**....

"**If any man will do his will, he shall know of the doctrine**, whether it be of God, or whether I speak of myself" John 7:17 (KJV).

If you are already saved, and you find yourself "**forever learning, but never coming to the knowledge of truth,**" be honest with yourself (and your Lord). Ask yourself, "Are you truly willing to do **all** of God's will in your life?" If the answer is yes, then the bible says you will understand the doctrines in the Word of God. If the answer is no, you **will not** know and understand the doctrines in the Word of God. It is that simple.

Too many pastors, too many priests, too many congregations, too many Christians are only willing to do part of God's will. This is why we have so much unlearned behavior and teaching in the church in America today.

Regardless of our willingness to do God's will, we were fearfully and wonderfully made in such a way as to desire the truth. We can be sure of this understanding because Almighty God desires truth to reside in our inward parts.

Psalms 51:6 (KJV) ⁶Behold, thou desirest truth in the **inward parts**: and in the hidden *part* thou shalt make me to know wisdom.

If you are not saved or simply are not sure of your salvation, pray to God. **Acknowledge** that you are a sinner. **Ask** Him to save you from your iniquities. Confess your sins before Him. You then will be saved. It's as easy as A-B-C! Simply **ASK-BELIEVE-CONFESS**.

Chapter 4

The Salvation Test

³How do we know if someone we care about is saved? Can we really know for sure?

Yes, we can know if a loved one is saved and this is how… **Test the spirit**. That is right, test the spirit. Is the spirit within the individual, of God, or of the antichrist? There are only two choices. This is the simplest test in scripture for determining immediately if a person is saved or not.

> 1 John 4:2-3 (KJV) "² Hereby **know ye the Spirit of God**: **Every spirit** that **confesseth** that Jesus Christ is come in the flesh **is of God**. ³ And every spirit that **confesseth not** that Jesus Christ is come in the flesh **is not of God**; and this is that **spirit of antichrist**, whereof ye have heard that it should come; and even now already is in the world."

There are many skeptics who think that this spiritual test cannot work. I was once a skeptic myself. Let's study 1 John 4:2-3 within its context so that we can conclude without any doubt that the precise intention of the scripture is for believers to "try" the spirit, meaning to test the spirit in individuals in order to determine to whom they belong:

First we must set the context of the passage, i.e. what is the scripture speaking about in the "Big Picture?"

> 1 John 4:1 (KJV) "¹Beloved, **believe not every spirit, but try the spirits** <u>whether they are of God</u>: because many false prophets are gone out into the world."

From verse 1 we know the passage is speaking directly to believers, the Apostle John addresses them as "Beloved." Next he commands them to believe NOT every spirit but **try** (meaning to test) them. John further gives us two reasons why we need to test the spirits. First, is to determine "whether they are of God" or not. Second, is "because many false prophets are gone out into the world." The spirits we are testing are men's, specifically false prophets. Notice how John directs us to test the spirit in men, not the man himself or his knowledge, there is a difference. One is spirit, the other is flesh, the spirit is eternal, and the flesh and mind are temporal.

When we ask an individual, "**Do you believe that Jesus Christ is come in the flesh?**" We are speaking directly to the spirit within the individual, not to his or her mind. We know from Luke 10:20 that the spirits (of men, angels and demons) are subject unto believers. They must answer us when we ask.

> Luke 10:20 (KJV) "²⁰Notwithstanding in this **rejoice** not, that <u>the spirits are subject unto you</u>; but rather **rejoice**, because your names are written in heaven."

This is a wonderful tool the Lord gives us here on earth to determine if a loved one is saved, and an important one indeed. A while ago I heard a pastor quote a poll taken among his fellow pastors in America, which indicated that 36% of clergy in America today DO NOT believe in the bodily resurrection of Jesus Christ. That tells me that the 36% who were polled, and take this position, are not saved. That could be your pastor or your priest! Would it be prudent of us to know if our pastor or priest is saved? What if he or she is a false prophet? Are we obligated to find out? Would knowledge of their salvation affect how we receive what they preach?

In America we trust our clergy in a way that greatly undermines the scripture, which teaches us to follow Christ, trust in His words, seek Him, etc.. Pastors and priests are overseers; the bible sometimes refers to them as bishops (1 Timothy 3). They are called by Almighty God to serve, not to be served as CEOs and Presidents of church businesses.

I have personally witnessed individuals, who confided in others and myself that they are Christians, and regularly attend church, who when asked this question: **"Do you believe that Jesus Christ is come in the flesh?"** have without hesitation said **NO**! Others have physically had their tongues tied by the Holy Spirit rendering them unable to confess a simple YES to this question. Still others go off on some unrelated tangent, while others cunningly ask off-topic questions as their response. Any answer, other than a YES, is equal to a NO! Try this test; you will be amazed how this simple question evokes an answer from a person's spirit, not their mind.

Ask a loved one whom you are unsure of their salvation…**"Do you believe that Jesus Christ is come in the flesh?"** Watch how they respond. If they don't answer, ask the exact same question again. Only an affirmative answer tells us someone has the Spirit of God inside, and not the spirit of antichrist inside. I trust you will be amazed how a person's spirit answers your question. Sometimes their spirit will answer "yes" immediately and a few moments later their mind starts wondering what did I say yes to?

I was golfing one day with a dear friend of mine who pastors a small church in Sedalia, Colorado. In fact, it was this pastor who first showed me 1 John 4:1-3. We were paired with Tom and John, two boys in their late teens. After learning that my friend was a pastor, Tom spent the next 17 holes telling my pastor friend and I about all the great things going on at his church. He spoke of many wonderful works that he himself was involved in. At one point in our conversation, Tom started quoting scripture, or maybe I should more accurately say he was mis-quoting scripture. Meanwhile John just listened in and absorbed the entire conversation, but he didn't say very much. I could tell he was listening very intently and his spirit was being stirred.

When Tom continued using scripture passages out of their context my friend and I started wondering what was wrong, we both knew something was just not right. Finally one of us asked Tom, "**Do you believe that Jesus Christ is come in the flesh?** His response to the questing was shocking. He said, "Uh, um, ahh, hmm, well, ah, …**NO!**" He literally mumbled for 10 or so seconds and then said NO! We couldn't believe it. He had just spent 17 holes telling us about what a great Christian he was, yet his spirit said NO, he was not even saved. In fact:

After the round of golf was finished, my pastor friend then explained to him that according to 1 John 4:1-3 his spirit was confessing that he was not saved. He then went on to invite him to pray a simple prayer of confession explaining that salvation was merely **believing** and **confessing** a personal belief that Jesus Christ is Lord, and God raised Him from the dead. Tom told my friend that he didn't want to commit to Jesus Christ today; maybe he would do it later. The real shocker came next:

Remember John? He was listening the entire time and when Tom rejected the opportunity to give his life to Jesus Christ, John felt the drawing of Almighty God to His Son Jesus Christ and he gave his life to Jesus Christ his new Lord, and the angels in heaven rejoiced. Another sinner came to repentance.

> John 6:44 (KJV) "⁴⁴* No man can come to me, except the Father which hath sent me <u>draw him</u>: and I will raise him up at the last day."

John was drawn to Jesus Christ the Lord on this fine day, amen.

> Luke 15:10 "¹⁰ Likewise, I say unto you, there is joy in the presence of the **angels** of God over one sinner that repenteth."

When we are ministering the Word of God, no matter where we are we never know who is listening, and who is not, we only recognize when the Spirit is moving.

Chapter 5

Salvation is Forever

⁴Can we ever lose our salvation? If so how? What must we do to keep it?

This is one of the least understood questions in the Christian world today… Can we lose our salvation? or stated another way, Once we are saved, are we always saved?

If there is any way to lose our salvation, then every one of us will indeed lose our salvation. Just ask Adam and Eve, they were born perfect, lived in a perfect Eden, yet found the one and only way to lose it all. We are no different.

No, we cannot lose our salvation. The devil will try to teach us differently, he even uses some modern American churches as his tool, but don't listen to them. He's a loser, and has already lost.

No, We cannot lose our Salvation

Reason # 1: We were bought with a price, we are no longer our own, but God's.

1 Corinthians 6:19-20 (KJV) "¹⁹ What? know ye not that your body is the temple of the Holy Ghost which is in you, which ye have of God, and ye are not your own? ²⁰ For ye are <u>bought with a price</u>: therefore glorify God in <u>your body</u>, and in <u>your spirit, which are God's</u>."

How can we lose something we no longer own? Once we accept the free and perfect gift we become bought with the price of Jesus Christ's' blood shed for us on the cross, we are no longer our own, we belong to Jesus Christ. Both our body and our spirit are now God's possession.

Reason # 2: We are a new creature, a spiritually transformed being.

2 Corinthians 5:17-18, 21 (KJV) "¹⁷ Therefore if any man be **in** Christ, <u>he is a new creature</u>: old things are passed away; behold, **all things are become new.** ¹⁸ And **all things are of God**, who hath reconciled us to himself by Jesus Christ, and hath given to us the ministry of reconciliation; ²¹ <u>For he (God the Father) hath made him (Jesus Christ) to be sin for us, who knew no sin; that we might be made the **righteousness of God** in him</u>."

At the moment of our salvation we became an entirely new creature. Our old sinful self has passed away. The word "in" from verse 17 is not a continuous, repeated action. Therefore there is nothing in the passage to suggest that we must keep getting saved over and over again. We still reside in our flesh; however, we are called to mortify the deeds of the body.

Romans 8:13 (KJV) "¹³ For if ye live after the flesh, ye shall die: but if ye through the Spirit do mortify the deeds of the body, ye shall live."

If the old creature has passed away, how can we go back to it? It's simple. We can't. Even if we want to go back, we are no longer our own possession, but that of God's (1 Corinthians 6:19-20). If we live after the flesh, the flesh will die, **not the spirit**.

Reason # 3: It is foolish to get saved over and over again (or to think we must get saved over and over), for it puts to shame the Son of God afresh.

1 Corinthians 1:21 (KJV) "²¹ For after that in the wisdom of God the world by wisdom knew not God, it pleased God by the <u>foolishness of preaching to</u> **save them that believe**."

It is foolishness to preach salvation to those who already believe because they are already saved. However, we must study the salvation message to come to unity in the understanding once saved, always and forever saved. We did nothing to earn our salvation, we can do nothing to lose it.

Hebrews 6: 4-6 (KJV) ⁴For *it is* impossible for those who were once enlightened, and have tasted of the heavenly gift, and were made partakers of the Holy Ghost, ⁵And have tasted the good word of God, and the powers of the world to come, ⁶If they shall fall away, to renew them again unto repentance; **seeing they crucify to themselves the Son of God afresh, and put *him* to an open shame**.

Here are some additional supporting references for further study, all of which point to eternal security for the believer:

- John 10: 26-28: "they shall never perish, neither shall <u>any man</u> pluck them out of my hand".
  If we can be plucked from God's hand, He's not providing much protection is He?

- 1 Peter 1: 3-5: "Who are <u>kept</u> by the power of God through faith **unto salvation**"
  If God can't keep us unto salvation He's not much of a God is He?

- Hebrews 7: 24-25: "Wherefore he is able also to save them <u>to the uttermost</u> that come unto God by Him, seeing He <u>ever liveth to make intercession</u> for them."
  If Jesus Christ is capable of saving us to the uttermost and He ever lives to make intercession for us and that's not enough, He's not much of an intercessor is He?

- Hebrews 10: 10-14: "For by one offering he hath <u>perfected for ever</u> them that are sanctified."
  If Jesus perfected forever the saved (sanctified, perfected) believer when are we not perfected?

- 2 Timothy 2: 11-13: "If we believe not, yet he abideth faithful: <u>he cannot deny himself</u>."
  Even if after we are saved we quit believing in Jesus, He cannot deny Himself, He is still faithful to save us in spite of ourselves.

- 1 John 5: 1, 1 John 3: 9: "Whosoever is born of God <u>doth not commit sin</u>;"
  Saved believers do not commit sin (spiritually), they are born of God (spiritually), so how can they lose their salva-

tion, which is spiritual? The flesh of course still sins, we must die to its deeds and desires.

∞ Philippians 1:6 "he which began a good work in you will perform it until the day of Jesus Christ"
God began the good work in us, it's up to Him to finish it!

⁵Is there anything else we must to do to be saved (be baptized, do good works, etc.)?

There is much division in the church concerning the doctrines of baptism and good works. In spite of the theological division, the answer to #5 is a resounding NO. Neither baptism, nor good works, nor anything else become prerequisites, or post-requisites for an individual to be saved or keep his or her salvation. Don't listen to satans lies, he loves to rob mankind of our rewards, and our crowns of righteousness.

Case and Point - The thief on the cross:

Luke 23: 39-43 (KJV) "³⁹ And one of the malefactors which were hanged railed on him, saying, If thou be the Christ, save thyself and us. ⁴⁰ But the other answering rebuked him, saying, Dost not thou fear God, seeing thou art in the same condemnation? ⁴¹ And we indeed justly; for we receive the due reward of our deeds: but this man hath done nothing amiss. ⁴² And <u>he said unto Jesus, Lord</u>, remember me when thou comest into thy kingdom. ⁴³ And Jesus said unto him, Verily I say unto thee, <u>Today shalt thou be with me in paradise</u>."

Is the thief saved? One would presume that being in paradise with Jesus is an affirming indication that he is saved.

The thief **confessed** with his mouth and **believed** in his heart that Jesus was Lord, and God would raise him from the dead, **thus he was saved** fulfilling Romans 10:9-10 from chapter 1. He had lived his entire life in darkness, apart from the goodness of Jesus Christ. From his own admission, he probably did few, if any good works, and he most certainly was not baptized. If salvation required anything outside of **belief** and **confession** it would have been recorded in this scripture for our benefit.

To say we must be baptized to be saved is to not understand what [1]water baptism and [2]spiritual baptism represent in the scriptures and in our lives:

> **1 water baptism (demonstrating a repentant heart)** - The Greek word (baptizo) means "to dip", "to immerse" or "to identify with". Water baptism is a **baptism of repentance** where we are confessing our desire to repent (to turn away) from our sinful nature and identify ourselves with the person of Jesus Christ. This response (a **repentant heart**) is a spiritual belief that happens inside our hearts and minds, and is confessed with our mouths, thus fulfilling the requirements of salvation (Romans 10:9-10). In fact, the believer taking part in the water baptism sacrament demonstrates a right conscience before both the brethren, and Almighty God.
>
> 1 Peter 3:21 (KJV)"[21]The like figure whereunto even baptism doth also now save us (not the putting away of the filth of the flesh, <u>but the answer of a **good conscience** toward God,</u>) by the resurrection of Jesus Christ:"

It is not the physical act in the ceremony that is of paramount importance; rather it is the confession of belief in Jesus Christ that demonstrates a "good conscience." Every Christian should be water baptized after their conversion, hence it is sometimes called the "first step of our faith." There are many reasons why every Christian should be water baptized, but perhaps Christ's example is the compelling one:

John 1:29-34(KJV) ²⁹The next day John seeth Jesus coming unto him, and saith, Behold the Lamb of God, which taketh away the sin of the world. ³⁰ This is he of whom I said, After me cometh a man which is preferred before me: for he was before me. ³¹ And I knew him not: but that he should be made manifest to Israel, therefore am I come baptizing with water. ³² And John bare record, saying, **I saw <u>the Spirit descending from heaven like a dove</u>**, and it abode upon him. ³³ And I knew him not: but he that sent me to baptize with water, the same said unto me, Upon whom thou shalt see the Spirit descending, and remaining on him, the same is he which baptizeth with the Holy Ghost. ³⁴ And I saw, and bare record that this is the Son of God.,

Matthew 3:13-17 (KJV) ¹³Then cometh Jesus from Galilee to Jordan unto John, to be baptized of him. ¹⁴ But John forbad him, saying, I have need to be baptized of thee, and comest thou to me? ¹⁵ And Jesus answering said unto him, Suffer *it to be so* now: for thus it becometh us to fulfill all righteousness. Then he suffered him. ¹⁶ And Jesus, when he was baptized, went up straightway out of the water: and, lo, the heavens were opened unto him, and **he saw <u>the Spirit of God descending like a dove</u>**, and lighting upon him: ¹⁷ And lo a voice from heaven, saying, This is my beloved Son, in whom I am well pleased.).

Luke 3:21-22 (KJV) **21** Now when all the people were baptized, it came to pass, that Jesus also being baptized, and praying, the heaven was opened, **22** And **the Holy Ghost descended in a bodily shape like a dove upon him**, and a voice came from heaven, which said, Thou art my beloved Son; in thee I am well pleased.

Notice in the three gospel accounts of Jesus' baptism, that "the Spirit (in John), the Spirit of God (in Matthew), and the Holy Ghost (in Luke)" all three are accounted as descending upon Jesus like a dove. Modern theologians assume that these three are one and the same and all three are in fact the third person of the trinity. A simple word study in the New Testament shows overlap between the three, but does not support a conclusion that all three are describing the third person of the trinity. We do know that Jesus Christ received "the Spirit" not by measure. He received more…the Spirit, the Spirit of God and the Holy Ghost. Could it be that somehow, some way "the Spirit" is of Jesus Christ, the "Spirit of God" is of the Father God and the "Holy Ghost" is the third person of the trinity? Is this what the scriptures refer to as a "full measure?"

John 3:34(KJV) "**34** For he whom God hath sent speaketh the words of God: for God giveth not the Spirit **by measure** unto Him."

Additionally, water baptism is the act of immersing the new believer in water as a testimony that he or she has experienced the reality of the conversion experience, and has been transformed from death to life. The sacrament is not to be equated with salvation. Specifically, it is an act of repentance or turning toward God the Father Almighty and away from sin. Paul does a wonderful job of explaining the symbolic significance of baptism in the

Book of Romans:

> Romans 6:3-6 (KJV) ³Know ye not, that so many of us as were baptized into Jesus Christ were baptized into his death? ⁴ Therefore we are buried with him by baptism into death: that like as Christ was raised up from the dead by the glory of the Father, even so we also should walk in newness of life. ⁵ For if we have been planted together in the likeness of his death, we shall be also *in the likeness* of *his* resurrection: ⁶ Knowing this, that our old man is crucified with *him*, that the body of sin might be destroyed, that henceforth we should not serve sin.

First, baptism represents death (Romans 6:3). Second, it represents redemption, picturing the gospel (Romans 6:4). Third, baptism represents our hope in a future resurrection (Romans 6:5). Fourth, baptism symbolizes our new life, the old life is crucified with Christ. We are no longer serving sin and we have a new master (Romans 6:6). Every believer should indeed be water baptized, but only of his own free will. This is our choice, not God's requirement, but surely His desire.

² spiritual baptism (an anointing for service) - Spiritual baptism is that which Luke first spoke about in the book of Acts. It is the baptism of the Holy Spirit as recorded in Acts 2:2-3. It is an account of the Holy Spirit moving upon the believer.

Spiritual baptism has both an internal and an external manifestation. The internal working of Spiritual baptism, or the infilling of the Holy Spirit, should be desired by all who desire to "walk in the Spirit" (Galatians 5:16). When a believer is in-filled by the Holy Spirit, the Holy Spirit empowers (Acts 1:8) the believer to witness to others (Acts 4:29-31). Like water baptism, there are many reasons why every Christian should desire spiritual baptism and it's internal working, the in-filling of the Holy Spirit, but Christ's example stands true (John 3:34-35).

Note: In the Old Testament, God sovereignly chose who was to receive the Holy Spirit. In the church age however, the Holy Spirit was poured out upon <u>all flesh</u> (Acts 2:17), but in-filled separately some <u>who asked</u> for the Holy Spirit (Luke 11:13), and some who <u>heard the Word</u> (Acts 8:14-17, 10:44-48).

In any case, neither water baptism, nor spiritual baptisms are requirements for salvation. However, salvation is a prerequisite to receive either baptism (John 14:17, Acts 2:38).

> Acts 1: 5, 8 (KJV) "*5* For John truly **baptized with water**; but <u>ye shall be **baptized with the Holy Ghost**</u> not many days hence. *8* But <u>ye shall **receive power**</u>, after that the Holy Ghost is <u>come upon you</u>: and <u>ye will **be witnesses**</u> unto me both in Jerusalem, and in all Judea, and in Samaria, and unto the uttermost part of the earth."

Two questions we should ask ourselves are:

#1 - Were the Apostles saved prior to their water baptism and spiritual baptism? Jesus explains the difference between the two baptisms (water and spiritual), one baptism with water for repentance, the other by the Holy Ghost yielding power for witnessing. Also, keep in mind that the Holy Ghost was to come <u>upon</u> them all, this is the external manifestation of the spiritual baptism.

> Acts 2:17 (KJV) "*17* And it shall come to pass in the last days, saith God, I will pour out of my Spirit **upon all flesh**: and your sons and your daughters shall prophesy, and your young men shall see visions, and your old men shall dream dreams:"

#2 - Were the apostles powerful witnesses prior to the arrival of the Holy Ghost? It seems that the scriptures portray the apostles as fearing for their lives shortly after Christ's death. They were only bold servants when He was here dwelling in the flesh, they were in hiding, fearing for their lives.

Interestingly enough, immediately after the Holy Spirit was poured out upon them He also in-filled them as was evidenced by their speaking in unknown tongues.

> Acts 2:4 (KJV) "⁴ And they were all **filled** with the Holy Ghost, and began to speak with other tongues, as the Spirit gave them utterance."

Next, let's look at the scriptures which might cause us to believe that baptism is necessary in order for one to receive salvation.

> John 3: 5-6 (KJV) "⁵ Jesus answered, Verily, verily, I say unto thee, <u>Except a man be born of water and of the Spirit, he cannot enter into the Kingdom of God</u>. ⁶ That which is born of the flesh is flesh; and that which is born of the Spirit is Spirit."

As we discovered earlier, to be "born of water" is not the physical act of water baptism, but the mindset of a repentant heart. Maybe this passage is speaking to physical birth (the breaking of the placenta holding water in the birthing process). Regardless, we must mentally repent and acknowledge our need for forgiveness of sins **before** we do anything about it.

To be "born of the Spirit" is the spiritual result of our repentance and desire to grow in God's grace. God gives us the gift of access to Him through prayer and empowers us with certain spiritual gifts to edify the body of Christ (1 Corinthians 12, Romans 12, Ephesians 4, 1 Peter 4). The external manifestation of spiritual baptism is the

Holy Spirit coming <u>upon</u> and being <u>available to</u> every saved believer. **This is not to be confused with the internal manifestation of the spiritual baptism, the infilling of the Holy Spirit.**

Truly this doctrine of Spiritual Baptism and it's internal working needs much time, prayer and study to understand in depth. Here are some additional supporting references for further study to help shed light on the sufficiency of Jesus Christ:

> ∞ Romans 4:1-8: "But to him that **worketh not**, <u>but believeth</u> on Him that justifieth the ungodly, <u>his faith is counted for righteousness</u>."

Even the believer who does no good work for the Kingdom is still saved, because his faith is counted for righteousness. This is a poor choice and could result in a believer living in "outer darkness" during the 1,000 year reign of Christ on earth.

> ∞ John 4:10-14: "but the water that I shall give him shall be in him a well of water springing up into everlasting life".
> Jesus Christ gives the water of life, all we do is drink it in.

> ∞ John 15:3-5: "Now ye are <u>clean through the word</u> which I have spoken unto you"
> We are made clean through the Word (Jesus Christ-John 1:1), not by our own efforts.

> ∞ Ephesians 5:25-27: "That he might sanctify and cleanse it with the washing of the water <u>by the word</u>,"
> The church is sanctified and cleansed by the Word (Jesus Christ), not by our own works.

∞ Titus 3:3-7: "Not by works of righteousness which we have done, but according to his mercy he saved us, by the washing of regeneration, and renewing of the Holy Ghost;"

Our own works have nothing to do with our salvation, but they have everything to do with our glory (1 Corinthians 15:41-42). We were saved according to the mercy of Christ not by our own works of righteousness.

∞ 1 Corinthians 3:11-15: "For other foundation can no man lay than that is laid, which is Jesus Christ."

Only Jesus Christ can lay the foundation of salvation, Himself.

∞ Ephesians 2:8-9: "For by grace are ye saved through faith: ⁹ Not of works, lest any man should boast."

Salvation is by the **grace of God** through the **faith of God**, not our own works or man would boast in himself.

Chapter 6

Are there scriptures that might lead us to a different conclusion? A right dividing of the Word of God for brethren with a heart for Truth.

If you have lasted through the first five chapters, I praise God for your heart seeking the Truth, I trust that the Holy Ghost has been teaching you some new and wonderful revelations from all the passages presented thus far. It has been a treasured time for me re-learning and discussing these scriptures and doctrines concerning our Lord Jesus Christ. I pray for many more such opportunities before the coming day of our Lord.

Before we look at the scriptures some believers use to form their belief that we can lose our salvation, let's look at one passage they can't reprove. **Do we have an example of a believer living an ungodly life yet the Word of God judges them as saved? See for yourself.**

> 1 Corinthians 5:1-6 (KJV) ¹ It is reported commonly *that there is* fornication <u>among you</u>, and such fornication as is not so much as named among the Gentiles, that one should have his father's

wife. ²And ye are puffed up, and have not rather mourned, that <u>he that hath done this deed might be taken away from among you</u>. ³For I verily, as absent in body, but present in spirit, have judged already, as though I were present, *concerning* him that hath so done this deed, ⁴In the name of our Lord Jesus Christ, when ye are gathered together, and my spirit, with the power of our Lord Jesus Christ, **⁵To deliver such an one unto Satan for the destruction of the flesh, <u>that the spirit may be saved</u> in the day of the Lord Jesus.** ⁶Your glorying *is* not good. Know ye not that a little leaven leaveneth the whole lump?

Four Key truths in 1 Corinthians 5:1-6:
1. The sin is in the church among the brethren.
2. The judgment in earth is to put the sinner away from the church.
3. The sinner is to be delivered to satan for the destruction of the flesh, not spiritual condemnation for eternity!
4. The spirit is SAVED in the day of the Lord Jesus! The purpose of his deliverance to satan is to LEARN, not to BURN in hell for eternity.

1 Timothy 1:18-20 ¹⁸This charge I commit unto thee, son Timothy, according to the prophecies which went before on thee, that thou by them mightest war a good warfare; ¹⁹Holding faith, and a good conscience; which some having put away concerning faith have made shipwreck: ²⁰Of whom is Hymenaeus and Alexander; whom **I have delivered unto Satan, that they may learn not to blaspheme.**

Once again, the purpose of their deliverance to satan is to LEARN, not to BURN in hell for eternity.

Let's review some scriptures that have been presented and

taught by others believed to be speaking about salvation.

To God be the Glory! Pray diligently to our Lord Jesus Christ asking Him to reveal scriptural truth as we study out each and every scripture. The following is a spiritual comparison and judgment concerning these scriptures and more:

> James 2:14 (KJV) "What doth it **profit**, my brethren, though a man **say** he hath faith, and have not works? **can faith save him**?"

This is one of the simplest, yet most misunderstood scriptures in all of the Word of God. Often when we read scripture it is very easy to take any one or two sentences out of their context, creating an unintentional representation of the scripture. Applying James 2:14 to salvation is a classic example of this error. In the written Word of God we must logically, and more importantly, spiritually discern the entire context, and the message. Spiritual discernment concerning doctrine comes from the Holy Spirit (John 7:17), **<u>only</u> if we will do God's will, not our own**. Let's spiritually discern James 2:14 (in other words, compare spiritual with spiritual, 1 Corinthians 2:13):

Questions we need to ask?
1. Who is the apostle James writing to?
2. What is the apostle James writing about?
3. What is God's message through the Apostle?

First, let's put scripture in its proper context: James is writing to Jews (James 1:1), <u>not Gentiles</u>. It seems there were some Jews at the time reacting to Paul's gospel inappropriately. **They were acting as if works played no part in the Christian's experience.**

Additionally, these were extremely immature Jewish believers, witness:

James, Chapter 1 - These Jews didn't understand trials, the

work of patience in ones life, and they didn't have wisdom to handle those trials due to their double mindedness (spirit-flesh). They also thought that God tempted them in fleshly ways and didn't understand that they were tempted of their own flesh and lusts. They were wrathful, and not doers of the Word of God (they were hearers only), and they didn't bridle their tongues.

James, Chapter 2 - They were respecters of persons and were legal in their thoughts. They spouted out that they had great faith, when in reality James had to rebuke them sharply that they had no fruit of their so-called faith. They were just "blow-hards", big talkers.

James, Chapter 3 - They seemed to want place or recognition, and to be teachers, but they were in no way qualified to teach. They spoke great things with their tongues and offended—James rebuked this error. They cursed and blessed from the same tongue, they envied, caused strife, and had no fruit of righteousness.

James, Chapter 4 - They prayed in error that they could consume it upon their lusts. They loved the world and were at enmity with God. They were proud, not humble, they resisted the leading of God. They simply wouldn't submit to God. They spoke evil of one another. They thought they were in control of their own destiny and would do their own will without consulting their Lord and Savior. They were boasters and they knew to do right, but did not do it.

James, Chapter 5 - They were "money grubbers" and seemed to have gained wealth fraudulently. They were not patient and would not suffer for the Lord. They made oaths that they could not keep. They didn't know what to do for the sick among them—that God would heal them. They didn't know that Prayer was powerful when it is righteous. **They didn't realize the importance of helping someone if they erred from the truth.**

Point #1 (James Chapters 1-5): All in all, the brethren James was speaking to demonstrated an incredible lack of maturity. They were babes in Christ! Just like most in the church in America today. A close examination of the first five chapters of James reveals that the subject is "immature" Jewish believers:

> James 2:14-17 (KJV) "**14What doth it profit**, my brethren, though a man **say** he hath faith, and have not works? can faith save him? 15If a brother or sister be naked, and destitute of daily food, 16And one of you say unto them, Depart in peace, be ye warmed and filled; notwithstanding ye give them not those things which are needful to the body; **what doth it profit**? 17Even so faith, if it hath not works, is dead, being alone."

Point #2 (James 2:14-17): Foremost, James is writing about **Profit, not Salvation**; the sentence in verse 14 is complete after "and have not works?"

The Greek word for **profit** means to "heap up, accumulate or benefit" (Strong's #3786, ophelos). Do we accumulate, or heap up salvation? Do we have to continually be saved over and over again? No, of course not.

James is asking what is the **profit or benefit** if a believer **says** he has faith, but no works to show for his faith. The answer is obvious...very little, if any. Profit or benefit doesn't come from talk, it comes from reliance on and commitment to Almighty God.

Point #3: The Greek text suggests not "can faith save him?" as it is written in English, but "can that faith save him?" The "**that**" James is referring to is found in the middle of verse 14. "though a man **say** he hath faith,". **Can that type of faith save him?** No, of course not. That type of faith neither saves nor benefits anyone.

Case and point: These immature Jewish believers would not have been saved had they had **that type** of faith when they first believed. James makes a stern warning of the consequences of **that**

type of faith; the warning is Death.

We must be very careful not to misinterpret this James 2:14 passage by only applying it to salvation, because to do so ignores the specific point of the text and creates chaos and division within the body. Moreover, such blatant disregard for the context of the scripture discounts the very Gospel we will be judged by: Paul's gospel.

> Romans 2:16 (KJV) "¹⁶In the day when God shall judge the secrets of men by Jesus Christ **according to my gospel**."

Without works, yet saved?

The Pauline epistles do a wonderful job of bringing to light this issue of good works, profit and reward providing a perfect compliment to James epistle. Let's walk through just a few passages:

> Romans 4:1-8 (KJV) "¹What shall we say then that Abraham our father, as pertaining to the flesh, hath found? ²For if Abraham were justified by works, he hath whereof to glory; but not before God. ³For what saith the scripture? **Abraham believed God, and it was counted unto him for righteousness. ⁴Now to him that worketh is reward not reckoned of grace, but of debt. ⁵But to him that worketh not, but believeth on him that justifieth the ungodly, his faith is counted for righteousness.** ⁶Even as David also describeth the blessedness of the man, unto **whom God imputeth righteousness without works**, ⁷Saying, Blessed are they whose iniquities are forgiven, and whose sins are covered. ⁸Blessed is the man to whom the Lord will not impute sin."

Three Key truths in Romans 4:1-8:
1. Abraham's Justification is not by works, but by **Belief** in God. Belief that God is!

2. Works are for **profit & rewards,** <u>not salvation</u>.
3. If we **believe** on Jesus Christ & **confess** with our mouth God raised him from the dead, **yet are without works,** we still receive our Salvation because God imputes righteousness, not man.

Is fruit necessary for salvation?

Matthew 7:15-20 (KJV) "¹⁵**Beware of false prophets**, which come to you in sheep's clothing, but inwardly they are ravening wolves. ¹⁶**Ye shall know them by their fruits.** Do men gather grapes of thorns, or figs of thistles? ¹⁷Even so every good tree bringeth forth good fruit; but a corrupt tree bringeth forth evil fruit. ¹⁸A good tree cannot bring forth evil fruit, neither can a corrupt tree bring forth good fruit. ¹⁹Every tree that bringeth not forth good fruit is hewn down, and cast into the fire. ²⁰**Wherefore by their fruits ye shall know them.**"

Three Key truths in Matthew 7:15-20:
1. Who is the passage talking about? False Prophets, NOT believers.
2. What is the message? We can know False Prophets from True Prophets by their fruit.
3. Key consideration? **How long does it typically take a fruit bearing tree to bear fruit? Answer:** Typically three plus years, sometimes longer. The tropical bamboo seed spends ~5-7 years in the ground, then it grows up to 80' in a single year. There is wonderful revelation in God's creation. Can we apply this to a believer's walk? You judge for yourself.

If they bear no fruit they are young (like young children-we would conclude the young are not teachers or prophets as is the case in the secular world, this is not the case for God's chosen, i.e. Jeremiah was possibly ~13 years old); if they bear evil fruit they are devils (evil); if they bear good fruit they are maturing believers.

Not all trees in creation are fruit bearing, nor do all believers bear fruit. Yet all have a purpose!

Not all believers will receive the same rank or position in the Kingdom of Heaven (1 Corinthians 15:22-23, Hebrews 11:35, 1 Corinthians 15:40-42, 1 Corinthians 3:8, 2 Corinthians 3:18). This place or rank in the resurrection will be a result of the works of righteousness of each individual.

Must we follow the law to be saved?

> 2 Corinthians 3:1-6 (KJV) "¹Do we begin again to commend ourselves? or need we, as some others, epistles of commendation to you, or letters of commendation from you? ²**Ye are our epistle written in our hearts, known and read of all men**: ³Forasmuch as ye are manifestly declared to be the epistle of Christ ministered by us, written not with ink, but with the Spirit of the living God; not in tables of stone, but in fleshly tables of the heart. ⁴And such **trust have we through Christ** to Godward: ⁵**Not that we are sufficient of ourselves to think any thing as of ourselves; but our sufficiency is of God**; ⁶Who also hath made us able ministers of the new testament; **not** of the letter, but of the Spirit: for **the letter killeth**, but the Spirit giveth life."

Four key points from 2 Corinthians 3:1-6
1. How could they know they are "epistles" of Christ? It was written in their hearts, evidenced by their good works (verse 2).
2. Good works demonstrate **trust** (verse 4) in Jesus Christ, which exceeds mere **belief** in Him.
3. Their good works were not sufficient, Jesus Christ is sufficient

(verse 5).
4. The law kills, the Spirit gives life because Jesus Christ fulfilled (completed) the law. We are merely beneficiaries of the Faith of Jesus Christ.

How should we live?

> **1 Peter 4:4-6 (KJV)** "⁴Wherein they think it strange that ye run not with them to the same excess of riot, speaking evil of you: ⁵Who shall give account to him that is ready to judge the quick and the dead. ⁶For this cause was the gospel preached also to them that are **dead** (those dead in trespasses and sin), that they might be judged according to men in the flesh, **but live according to God in the spirit**."

Our call is to live according to the will of God, i.e. do good works, worship Him in spirit and in truth, and walk in the spirit. We **should be** good stewards of Gods grace, but certainly all believers are not good stewards of the grace given them.

How should we not live?

> **Titus 1:15-16 (KJV)** "¹⁵Unto the pure **all things** are pure: but unto them that are defiled and unbelieving **is nothing pure**; but even their mind and conscience is defiled. ¹⁶They **profess** that they know God; but in works they deny Him, being abominable, and disobedient, and unto every good work reprobate (disqualified, or worthless)."

Three key points to Titus 1:15-16:
1. Paul again compliments James 2:14. All is pure to the pure (verse 15).

2. These **false teachers** disqualify themselves from what? From salvation? No, they are disqualified from the race. They are not running the race by God's will and authority, they are running on their own (Hebrews 12:1, 1 Corinthians 9:24, 2 Timothy 4:7), and thus they will not receive a full reward. Just like the James 2:14 passage, there is no profit or benefit in his or her walk.
3. **We do not qualify for salvation, Jesus Christ qualified for us**. So how can we be "disqualified" from that which we are not qualified for in the first place? This scripture must not be speaking about salvation. It is speaking to good works for rewards.

Titus 2:11-14 (KJV) "¹¹For the grace of God that bringeth salvation hath appeared to all men, teaching us that, **denying ungodliness and worldly lusts, we <u>should</u> live soberly, righteously, and godly, in this present world**; looking for that blessed hope, and the glorious appearing of the great God and our Savior Jesus Christ; who gave himself for us, that He **might redeem us from all iniquity**, and **purify unto himself** a peculiar people, **zealous of good works**.

Jesus Christ purifies us to Himself, we do not purify ourselves through our good works. We are redeemed from iniquity and purified to God by Jesus Christ in us.

Paul once again compliments James call to good works. He does not however tie the good works to our salvation.

Are we justified by our works?

Titus 3:3-8 (KJV) "For we ourselves also were sometimes **foolish, disobedient, deceived, serving divers lusts and pleasures,** living in malice and envy, hateful, and hating one another. But after that the kindness and love of God our Savior toward man appeared, <u>**Not by works of righteousness which we have done**</u>, **but according to <u>his mercy</u> he saved us**, by the washing of regeneration, and renewing of the Holy Ghost; which He shed on us abundantly through Jesus Christ our Savior; **that being justified by His grace**, we should be made heirs according to the hope of eternal life. **This is a faithful saying, and these things I will that thou affirm constantly, that they which have believed in God might be careful to maintain good works. These things are <u>good and profitable</u>** unto men."

Again Paul encourages us to be careful to maintain good works, not for salvation, but for **profit and rewards**.

Good works are "good and profitable", they are not a requisite of salvation.

Can our works be worthless and our salvation assured?

> 1 Corinthians 3:11-15 "For other foundation can **<u>no man</u>** lay than that is laid, **which is Jesus Christ**. Now <u>**if any man**</u> build upon this foundation gold, silver, precious stones, wood, hay, stubble; Every man's work shall be **made manifest**: for the day shall declare it, because it shall be revealed by fire; and the fire shall try every man's work of what sort it is. **If any man's work abide which he hath built thereupon, <u>he shall receive a reward</u>. If any man's work shall be burned, he shall suffer loss:** but he <u>himself shall be saved</u>; yet so as by fire."

Five key points to 1 Corinthians 3:11-15:
1. <u>No man</u> can lay the foundation of salvation, only Jesus Christ.

2. <u>Any man</u> can build upon the foundation with works ranging from the precious and rare which are refined by the fire to the worthless, which burns in the fire and are consumed.
3. It is our works that are tried by fire, **not our salvation**.
4. Works that endure shall receive a reward.
5. If our works do not endure, we shall suffer loss of a reward, <u>not the loss of our salvation</u>.

Why do we labor?

> **2 Corinthians 5:9-10 (KJV)** "Wherefore we **labor**, that, whether present or absent, we may be **accepted** of Him. **For we must all appear before the judgment seat of Christ**; that every one **may receive** the things done in his body, according to that he hath done, whether it be good or bad."

We are not judged for salvation, we are judged of our works for rewards or lack thereof.

> **1 Corinthians 5:11-13 (KJV)** "But now I have written unto you not to keep company, if any man that is called **a brother** be a **fornicator, or covetous, or an idolater, or a railer, or a drunkard, or an extortioner**; with such a one, no, not to eat. For what have I to do to judge them also that are without? **do not ye judge them that are within? But them that are without God judgeth**. Therefore put away from among yourselves that wicked person."

Point #1: Who is Paul writing about? A saved person, a brother in Christ.

Point #2: What is the message? If a saved person is knowingly sinning it is our responsibility to put him out from among us so that

God may deal with him. He does not however, lose his salvation. His actions will cost him rank and rewards in the Kingdom of Heaven and in the Kingdom of God, not his salvation.

Point #3: Remember, when we were first called by God the Father Almighty to come to Jesus Christ his Son (John 6:44), we became babes in Christ (1 Corinthians 3:1-3). If babes, then what good works can babes do? **None, they have no capacity to do good works, yet their childlike faith can be a saving example to others**. Good works and Childlike faith **ARE NOT** the same thing! Babes in Christ are in constant need of food (spiritual food, the Word of God) and nurturing (by maturing believers). They are helpless and will die of spiritual starvation if left to their own accord.

Point #4: If works are a requisite of salvation <u>nobody</u> is going to heaven, because <u>nobody will be saved!</u> Look at the Jews as our example, they could not keep the law without sin, nor can we do good works without sin. The Bible states that in this flesh dwelleth no good thing (Romans 7:18) How can we do good works when evil is present with us (in our flesh) when we do them? We can't, because we are always sinful in either deed, or thought, or motive, our good works would be unacceptable and an abomination in the sight of the Lord. Praise Jesus Christ for relieving us of this burden and curse.

Point #5: We are all called to different callings (Ephesians 4:11-13), all for the same purpose however; to build up the body of our Lord Jesus Christ (1 Corinthians 12). All are called by God, but for different ministries (1 Corinthians 7:17-24). All believers have been engaged to marry Jesus Christ by Paul (2 Corinthians 11:2), this is a high calling (Philippians 3:14), but all believers will not chose to marry Him.

Point #6: The Holy Spirit searches our hearts and knows whether or not each individual will respond to any calling high or otherwise. Many will not respond, thus refusing their Lord and Savior. No matter what our calling we are to respond with gratitude (Colossians 3:12-17) and thanksgiving (1 Thessalonians 5:16-18).

Conclusion: Good works will indeed be a natural result or outworking of a maturing believer's walk; they are not however a requisite of salvation. They simply do not provide a determination of one's salvation.

Here are some other scriptures given as support to salvation by grace through faith alone, not by good works:

> Hebrews 7:24-25 (KJV) "But this man (Jesus Christ), because He continueth ever, hath an unchangeable priesthood. Wherefore He is able to save them (the world) **to the uttermost** that come unto God by Him (Jesus Christ), seeing He ever liveth to make intercession for them (those who come to God by Him, after salvation)."

From the very moment of our salvation Jesus Christ Himself makes intercession for us every time our flesh sins (Romans 7). How then, if Jesus Christ intercedes for us once we are saved (Hebrews 7:24-25) can we lose our salvation? **Does His interceding stop for those who are not walking a worthy walk?** Does He only intercede when our faith reaches some magical point where it is considered "saving faith" verses "non-saving" faith? No, the scripture says He is able to save those who come to him to the uttermost. That is from the time we first believe in our hearts and confess with our mouths (Romans 10:9-10, 13).

2 Timothy 2:13 (KJV) "If we **believe not** (are faithless after salvation), **yet he abideth faithful: he cannot deny himself**."

Jesus Christ is faithful to save us even when we are faithless. He still abides faithful and saves us from our own flesh. Praise His Name.

Ephesians 2:8-9 (KJV) "For **by grace** are ye **saved through faith**; and that not of yourselves: **it is the gift of God: not of works**, lest any man should boast."

This scripture is as clear as it gets. We are not saved by works or man would boast.

Galations 2:16 (KJV) "Knowing that a **man is not justified by the works of the law, but by the faith of Jesus Christ**, even we have **believed** in Jesus Christ, that we might be **justified** from **the curse of the law**, being made a curse for us: for it is written: Cursed is everyone that hangeth on a tree."

We are justified by the faith of Jesus Christ, **not our faith**. We do not have so much faith as that of a mustard seed (Matthew 17:20). At least I haven't seen any "great faith" Christians moving any mountains recently - spiritual mountains or otherwise!

Romans 10:4 (KJV) "For Christ is the **end of the law** for righteousness **to every one that believeth**."

Jesus Christ put an end to the law of works required for salvation. There is no longer a need to establish our own righteousnes, Jesus did this for us.

Spiritual Truth

We do not do good works....God the Father Almighty does good works through Christ in us!

We do not do good works....God the Father Almighty does good works through Christ in us!

We do not do good works....God the Father Almighty does good works through Christ in us!

We do not do good works....God the Father Almighty does good works through Christ in us!

We do not do good works....God the Father Almighty does good works through Christ in us!

God sees our heart, men judge us by our outward appearance.....Therefore, good works are a necessary part of a maturing believers walk under our call to witness to non-believers and believers alike (Matthew 28: 19-20).

New questions to examine and study:
1. What happens after salvation? What can we expect?
2. What do we do next, after salvation?
3. What happens to us the moment we are saved?
4. Can and should we share our newfound faith with others?
5. Is salvation the ultimate hope for man, or is there more?

Jesus Christ invites us all to quit Swimming in the Lukewarm Waters of Compromise, come out, be separate and find joy in the Living Waters of Jesus Christ our Great God and Savior!

Endnotes

1. In Christian homes across the world, the King James Version of the Holy Bible is central, forming the basis of living. It defines the marriage, guides the maturity and growth of our families, and educates every member of the family. For the committed student of the Scriptures, we recommend the *Hebrew-Greek Key Word Study Bible* – King James Version only (Published 1991 by AMG International, Inc.).
2. When studying the Word of God, it is important to look up definitions of certain words in the Hebrew or Greek. Since the Old Testament was originally written in Hebrew and the New Testament was originally written in Greek, it is often helpful to return to the original language to see the meaning of the word. The best study tool we have found to help you study the scriptures in a deeper level is *The New Strong's Exhaustive Concordance of the Bible* (Published 1990 by Thomas Nelson Publishers). In the opinion of this author, newer versions of this concordance have been watered down and compromised, be careful.
3. In homes that value education, the dictionary has an important role in the intellectual growth of the family. Does your dictio-

nary reinforce and verify Bible study for your family, or does it introduce conflicting values and a secular world view? Our recommendation is the *American Dictionary of the English Language* (Published originally by Noah Webster in 1828, now by the Foundation for American Christian Education).

4. For the purposes of this book we quoted definitions of certain words using the *Nelson's Illustrated Bible Dictionary* (Published by Thomas Nelson Publishers in 1986).

5. For a better understanding of the difference between Christianity and at least 20 other worldviews please find a copy of *So What's the Difference* by Fritz Ridenour (Published in 2001 by Regal Books).

6. For an exhaustive documentation exposing the message, men and manuscripts moving mankind to the antichrist's one world religion a must study is *New Age Bible Versions* by G.A. Riplinger (Published in 1993 by A.V. Publications Corporation).